96 0997

DATE DUE

JUN 2 4 1996	
JAN 1 4 1997	
SEP 2 4 1997	
MAY 2 2 1998	
DEC 2 8 2000	
APR 1 1 2001	
JUL 2 6 2001	
FEB 1 2 2002	
SEP 0 5 2002	
SEP 0 5 2002	
OCT 0 7 2003	
NOV 0 7 2005	

GAYLORD

PRINTED IN U.S.A.

D0368608

Truck and Tractor Pulling

Jeff Savage

Capstone Press
MINNEAPOLIS

Printed in the United States of America.

Capstone Press • 2440 Fernbrook Lane • Minneapolis, MN 55447

Editorial Director   John Coughlan
Managing Editor   John Martin
Production Editor   James Stapleton

Photo Credits: John Brasseaux: pp. 4, 6-7, 8, 10, 15, 18, 22, 24, 28, 30, 32, 34, 36, 38, 39, 40; Larry Buche: pp. 12, 27.

Library of Congress Cataloging-in-Publication Data

Savage, Jeff, 1961--
    Truck and tractor pulling / by Jeff Savage
        p. cm. -- (Motorsports)
    Includes bibliographical references and index.
    ISBN 1-56065-260-8
    1. Tractor driving--Competitions--Juvenile literature.
  2. Truck driving--Competitions--Juvenile literature. [1.
Tractor driving--Competitions. 2. Truck driving--
Competitions.] I. Title. II. Series.
  TL233.3.S28   1996
  796.7--dc20   95-7353
                                              CIP
                                              AC

99 98 97 96 95   6 5 4 3 2 1

Table of Contents

Chapter 1
A Great Tractor Pull

John Powell drives to the starting line in
Rolling Thunder. He revs the four engines on
the red tractor. The engines sputter as race
officials hook a heavy sled to the back of the
tractor. The **sled operator** takes his place at the
sled's controls. John is ready to go.

He's competing in the World Truck and
Tractor Pulling Finals. More than 35,000 fans
are watching the big event in the Houston
Astrodome.

The **flagman** drops the green flag. The
tractor's engines thunder as John squeezes hard
on the throttle.

Slowride pops a wheelie as the skid plate digs in deeper.

Rolling Thunder charges forward, dragging the heavy sled behind it. As the operator moves weight forward on the sled, the **skid plate** sinks into the dirt. The tractor pulls harder and begins to slow.

Rolling Thunder moves forward a little more. Now it's moving by inches. Finally, it pushes across the finish line. It has completed a **full pull.**

The Competition

Seven tractors remain. If any of them can make a full pull, there will be a **pull-off** against *Rolling Thunder*. If they can't, Powell will be the champion.

One by one, the tractors move down the track. One by one, they fail to make it to the finish line. With two tractors left to go, *Rolling Thunder* is the only vehicle to have made a full pull.

John Powell watches the action from the pit area. *Ohio Gold* is next. The sled's weight is too much for John Hileman's yellow, black, and gold tractor. Hileman stops short of the finish line.

Dusty Goes Last

Dusty Arfons is the final competitor. Her tractor, *Dragon Lady*, is a red machine powered by two jet engines. It jumps off the starting line.

Tractors kick up a lot of noise and dirt along the track.

As the sled gets heavier, *Dragon Lady* keeps going. The red tractor advances slowly. The jet engines roar as Dusty squeezes the throttle. John Powell looks up just in time to see *Dragon Lady* cross the finish line. Powell sees that there's going to be a pull-off.

The Pull-Off

Powell goes first. He drives *Rolling Thunder* to the starting line and waits for the green flag. The flag falls and he takes off. The sled is heavier than on the first pull. *Rolling Thunder* powers its way 250 feet (76 meters) down the track.

Arfons takes her position at the starting line with *Dragon Lady*. She knows the distance she has to beat. The flagman gives the signal, and *Dragon Lady* begins rolling. The red tractor hauls the sled right past John's 250-foot (76-meter) mark. *Dragon Lady* doesn't stop until it goes 270 feet (82 meters). The crowd cheers wildly. Dusty Arfons is the world-champion tractor puller.

Chapter 2
Pulling

T ruck and tractor pulling is different from other motorsports. It takes power and balance–not speed–to win.

Motorized pulling began in 1929, when a group called the *Blue Shirts* sponsored an event at Bowling Green, Ohio. In 1969, the National Tractor Pullers Association was formed. This organization wrote the rules followed in nearly all pulling competitions.

Every year there are more than 500 indoor and outdoor pulling events in the United States and Canada. Thousands of fans pack the stadiums and arenas to see the powerful trucks and tractors compete.

Registration

To compete in a pulling event, drivers must first register their vehicles. Officials weigh each vehicle to determine its weight class. They include the driver and fuel in the total weight.

A lottery determines the pulling order. Drivers draw numbered balls from a spinning cage. The driver who draws the lowest-numbered ball goes first. The next-lowest number goes second, and so on.

The Test Puller

The first driver is the **test puller**. The test puller determines if the sled is a good weight for pulling. If he or she makes an easy full pull, the sled operator can make the sled heavier. If the test puller can't move the sled, the operator can lighten it. The test puller can then make a second pull.

Semitrailer trucks have the raw power to pull any sled.

Winning

In truck and tractor pulling, the vehicle that pulls the sled farthest is the winner.

When the sled comes to a stop, judges measure the distance it has traveled. If the front of the sled crosses the finish line, the driver has made a full pull. Drivers call this "going out the door" or "moving out the barn." If only one driver makes a full pull, he or she wins. If two or more drivers do it, there has to be a pull-off.

In a pull-off, the vehicle that pulls the sled farthest wins. If more than one vehicle makes another full pull, the drivers compete in more pull-offs until only one or neither can make a full pull.

Repulls

Many things can go wrong in a pull. The vehicle's front tires may lift too high, for example. This makes it impossible to pull the sled. The **throttle** may jam. Or the vehicle may go out of control and head toward the out-of-bounds line. If any of these things happen, the driver can signal for a **repull**.

The driver cannot wait until the end of the pull to ask for a repull. He or she must signal before the vehicle travels 75 feet (23 meters). A driver makes the signal by waving to the flagman at the finish line. The rules allow only one repull.

Track Officials

Officials carefully observe the pulling competition. One flagman stands at the starting line to signal the start of the race. A second flagman is at the finish line. The sled operator stands on top of the sled. He controls the weight of the sled by moving its weight box forward.

There are judges who measure the distance pulled. There are also track officials who watch the boundary lines. If a vehicle crosses the out-of-bounds line, it is disqualified.

Chapter 3

The Sled

In the 1930s, farmers entered their tractors in **tug pulls** at local fairs. They took turns pulling a heavy plate of steel with their tractors. Judges added more and more boulders to the plate until only one tractor could pull it.

Trucks began to participate in the pulling contests in the 1950s. These competitions featured a **step-on sled**. As the vehicle pulled the step-on sled down the track, men would get on the sled every ten feet or so (about three meters) until the sled would go no further.

The wheeled sled came into use in the 1960s. It had four back tires and a small weight box. While the truck or tractor pulled the wheeled sled, men would add steel and concrete blocks to the weight box. It was hard work.

The Modern Sled

Today's sled is a large machine with moveable weights. It is sometimes called a **weight transfer machine**. It can weigh as much as 33 tons (30 metric tons). It is also easier to work than earlier sleds. Nobody needs to step on it or to handle heavy weights.

On a modern sled, a weight box containing huge steel or concrete blocks sits at the back of the sled. As the sled moves, the operator uses a series of pulleys on a chain drive to move the box forward. This makes the sled heavier.

On the front of the sled is a steel plate called a pan or **skid plate**. As the weight box shifts forward, the steel plate sinks into the ground. As the plate digs deeper, it gets tougher for the truck or tractor to pull the sled.

Adjusting the Sled

If the test puller makes an easy full pull, or if there is a pull-off, the sled operator can make the sled heavier. A forklift can place concrete slabs in the weight box. Or the sled operator can shift gears to move the weight box forward at a faster rate. An operator can use both methods to make the sled extra heavy.

Safety

A sled must have certain safety features in order to be used in a pulling competition. It must have its own brakes. It also has to have a **kill switch**. This switch shuts off the engine of the pulling vehicle if it breaks free from the sled. Each year an inspector from the North American Sled Operators Association examines the sleds to make sure they are in good, safe working order.

Chapter 4
Trucks and Tractors

The two kinds of pulling vehicles are trucks and tractors. These compete in several weight and size classes. (Trucks never compete against tractors.) Trucks and tractors always compete against vehicles in the same weight and size class.

Pulling Tractors

The four types of pulling tractors are super stock, pro stock, modified, and modified mini.

Super Stock Tractors

Super stock tractors are farm tractors made by companies like John Deere, Case

Modified tractors can kick up more than 2,000 horsepower.

International, Massey-Ferguson, and International Harvester. They have modified engines with as many as four turbochargers. These engines can produce over 2,000 horsepower. They generate a wheel speed of nearly 80 miles (129 kilometers) per hour.

Super stock tractors can use either diesel fuel or alcohol fuel. They are sometimes called **smokers** because they belch black smoke into the air. The three weight classes for super stock tractors are 5,500 pounds (2,492 kilograms), 7,500 pounds (3,402 kilograms), and 9,500 pounds (4,309 kilograms).

Pro Stock Tractors

Pro stock tractors are super stock tractors that have only one turbocharger and can use only diesel fuel. They can weigh as much as 10,000 pounds (4,536 kilograms).

Modified Tractors and Modified Mini Tractors

Modified tractors are the loudest and most powerful vehicles in motorsports. They have small front wheels, long bodies, and huge rear wheels. They have as many as six engines, each with its own alcohol fuel tank. These vehicles can achieve wheel speeds up to 140 miles (225 kilometers) per hour. Modified tractors weigh as much as 11,200 pounds (5,080 kilograms).

Modified mini tractors are small modified tractors. They are only 10 feet (3.3 meters) long and 6 feet (1.8 meters) wide. They weigh just 1,800 pounds (816 kilograms).

Pulling Trucks

There are three kinds of pulling trucks. These are four-wheel-drive trucks, two-wheel-drive trucks, and semitrailer trucks.

Four-Wheel-Drive Trucks

In a four-wheel-drive truck, the engine powers all four wheels. To get maximum traction, the front wheels are weighted with up to 500 pounds (226 kilograms) of extra weight.

Four-wheelers have alcohol-burning engines and weigh up to 6,200 pounds (2,812 kilograms). Chevrolet, Dodge, and Ford are the most common makes of pulling trucks.

Two-Wheel-Drive Trucks

Two-wheel-drive engines power only the rear wheels. Like tractors, two-wheelers perform best with their wheels up.

A '59 Chevy pickup blasts down the track.

Two-wheel-drive trucks can be anything
from a Model-T bucket to a Thunderbird or a
Chevy C-Cab. Many of them are made of
fiberglass. A popular engine is the alcohol-
burning Arias. Like the four-wheel-drive
pulling truck, two-wheelers are limited to
6,200 pounds (2,812 kilograms).

The green flag is out for this powerful semitrailer truck.

Four-wheelers and two-wheelers may look street legal, but they are high-performance machines. It is illegal to drive them on the street.

Semitrailer Trucks

Semitrailer trucks compete in the newest division of pulling trucks. These trucks are usually called "semis."

Semis do not have the wheel speed of other pulling vehicles. But they have the raw power to pull any sled. The trucks can weigh over 20,000 pounds (9,072 kilograms). Some popular semi makes are Mack, Kenworth, and Peterbilt.

Tires

Most pulling trucks use Firestone, Goodyear, or BF Goodrich tires. To get maximum traction, drivers cut away tire tread with a wheel grinder.

Different pullers use different tread depths on their tires. Some like their tires' treads as shallow as one-half inch (1.3 centimeter). There are professional tire cutters whose job it is to make specially designed puller tires.

Chapter 5
The Track

In pulling contests, a lot depends on the track. Competitors have little chance of making a full pull on a bad track.

A good pulling track has just the right amounts of dirt and water. If the track is too dry, the skid plate will not sink into the ground. If it is too wet, the pulling vehicle's tires will have no traction.

Outdoor Tracks and Indoor Tracks

There are both outdoor tracks and indoor tracks. They differ from each other in several important ways.

A track official signals the driver to begin his pull. Driver and sled operator watch him closely.

All outdoor tracks are 300 feet (91 meters) long from start to finish. To build one, workers churn up and smooth out the ground. They add fresh dirt if necessary.

Indoor tracks range from 200 to 270 feet (61 and 82 meters) long. As much as 750 cubic yards (573 cubic meters) of compact clay dirt is brought into the arena. The dirt goes directly on the cement floor or a plywood surface. Modified tractors need at least a foot of dirt for pulling.

It takes plenty of heavy equipment to build a track. Bulldozers, rollers, rubber-tired loaders, grading tractors, power harrows, and back hoes arc uscd. During the competition, officials keep the surface smooth with a grader.

Drivers call the ideal track a **power track.** A power track is packed down hard and level, with no rough spots. Pullcrs perform best on a power track.

Chapter 6

The Drivers and the Circuit

Many drivers have full-time jobs. They might be farmers, mechanics, electricians, or secretaries. One driver quit his job as a college professor to become a full-time puller.

Some drivers began pulling as soon as they got their driver's license. And some continue pulling past age 65. Most pullers are men, but more women are pulling each year.

Driving Strategy

It takes more than raw horsepower to win a pull. Good driving skill is needed.

The engine of a pulling vehicle won't perform to the limit if the driver doesn't squeeze hard enough on the throttle. But squeezing too hard might lift the front end too high in the air. It takes skill to handle the throttle just right.

Smart drivers examine the track before their pulls. They watch what happens to the vehicles that run before them. Then they decide how to make their pass–down the left side, the right side, or the center of the track.

The Sport's Major Events and Circuits

The biggest events in truck and tractor pulling include the World Finals at the Houston Astrodome, the Indy Super Pull at the Indiana State Fairgrounds, and a three-day competition at Bowling Green, Kentucky. But there are important pulling competitions throughout the United States and Canada.

There are several pulling **circuits** up and running. A circuit is a group of events held at different locations during a single season. The National Tractor Pullers Association, USA

This modified tractor has a lot of noisy engine for the puller.

Motorsports, American Truck Puller, and SRO Motorsports sponsor circuit events throughout the United States and Canada. Each circuit has its own points system and prize money.

Points and Prizes

During the year, each driver earns points based on his or her finishes at pulling competitions.

These points are totaled after the last race of the circuit. The driver with the most points wins the overall championship of the pulling circuit. Winning drivers win prize money as well as points at each event. They win as much as $10,000 in a single competition. They also win prize money at the end of the circuit if they have a high number of overall points.

A John Deere tractor spits black smoke as its engine strains to pull the weights.

Chapter 7
Safety

W inning is not the most important thing in pulling. Both drivers and promoters will tell you there is something more important than winning. That is safety.

Precautions

Pullers know that crashes do happen. So they do everything possible to keep from getting hurt in a crash.

They wear helmets to protect their heads. The helmets' hard plastic material, called **Kevlar**, makes it tougher than a football helmet.

Pulling vehicles sometimes catch fire. A fireproof sheet of metal between the engine and driver serves as protection. Pulling vehicles must also have a fire extinguisher in the cab. Drivers guard against burns by wearing fireproof suits made of **flame-retardant** cotton.

Every driver wears a seat belt and a **shoulder harness**. In a crash, the belt and harness keep the driver in the seat.

Pulling vehicles usually have **roll bars**. A roll bar is a solid metal piece that goes above and around the cab of the vehicle. If the vehicle rolls over, the roll bar keeps the roof from collapsing.

Safety Crews

A medical crew and a fire crew are at every race. The medical crew consists of two licensed emergency medical technicians in an ambulance. The fire crew includes four officials who operate the fire equipment.

When a vehicle crashes, these crews rush to the scene. The medical crew helps the driver. If a fire breaks out, the fire crew quickly puts it out with extinguishers and fire hoses.

Glossary

chassis–the steel-tubed bars on which the vehicle's body sits. It is also called a frame.

circuit–a series of events in which points are awarded

flagman–an official who signals the start and end of a race and watches the boundary lines

flame retardant–material specially designed to keep from catching fire

full pull–when the front of the sled is pulled across the finish line. It is also known as "going out the door" or "moving out the barn."

Kevlar–hard plastic material used to make protective helmets

kill switch–a device that shuts off the pulling vehicle if it breaks free from the sled

pit area–the area where the pullers prepare their vehicles for the pull

power track–an ideal track that is packed down hard with no rough spots

pull-off–a contest in which two or more pullers who made a full pull compete to determine a winner

repull–a second pull awarded a driver who signals for it before his vehicle has traveled more than 75 feet (23 meters)

roll bar–a protective bar (usually a steel pipe) above and around the driver that prevents the vehicle from collapsing

shoulder harness–a protective belt that extends across a driver's chest from shoulder to lap

skid plate–a plate of steel on the front of the sled. It is also called a pan.

sled box–the part of the sled in which weights are placed

sled operator–an official who stands atop the sled and controls its weight by changing gears to advance the weight box

smokers–super stock farm tractors that belch smoke into the air

step-on sled–a metal plate on which men step to add weight

test puller–the first puller in a race. The sled operator adjusts the weight of the sled according to the performance of the test puller.

throttle–a device usually located on the steering wheel or dashboard that controls the amount of fuel sent from the tank to the cylinder

tug pulls–tractor-pulling contests held by midwestern farmers in the 1930s

weight transfer machine–a large machine with moveable weights used in modern pulling competitions

To Learn More

Atkinson, E.J. *Monster Vehicles*. Mankato, MN: Capstone Press, 1991.

Holder, Bill and Harry Dunn. *Monster Wheels*. New York: Sterling Publishing, 1990.

Johnson, Scott. *Monster Truck Racing*. Minneapolis: Capstone Press, 1994.

————. *The Original Monster Truck: Bigfoot*. Minneapolis: Capstone Press, 1994.

Savage, Jeff. *Demolition Derby*. Minneapolis: Capstone Press, 1995.

————. *Monster Truck Wars*. Minneapolis: Capstone Press, 1995.

————. *Mud Racing*. Minneapolis: Capstone Press, 1995.

Sullivan, George. *Here Come the Monster Trucks*. New York: Cobblehill Books, 1989

Some Useful Addresses

National Mud Racing Organization (NMRO)
5542 State Rt. 68 South
Urbana, OH 43078

National Tractor Pulling Association (NTPA)
6969 Worthington-Galena Road, Suite L
Worthington, OH 43085

SRO Motorsports
477 E Butterfield Road
Suite 400
Lombard, IL 60148

USA Motorsports
2310 W 75th Street
Prairie Village, KS 66208

Index